THE MAGIC BUS
AT THE
WATERWORKS

THE MAGIC BUS
AT THE WATERWORKS

By Joanna Cole   Illustrated by Bruce Degen

GUILD PUBLISHING
LONDON · NEW YORK · SYDNEY · TORONTO

The author and illustrator wish to thank Nancy Zeilig and
the technical services staff at American Water Works Association,
Denver, Colorado, for their help in preparing this book.

This edition published 1990 by Guild Publishing by arrangement with
Kingfisher Books, Grisewood & Dempsey Ltd,
Elsley House, 24–30 Great Titchfield Street,
London W1P 7AD

Originally published in USA by SCHOLASTIC INC.

CN 4895

Designed by Diana Hrisinko
Printed in Spain

To Rachel

J.C.

*For Uncle Jerry,
the Water Chemist*

B.D.

Our class really has bad luck.
This year, we got Ms Frizzle,
the strangest teacher in school.

We don't mind Ms Frizzle's strange dresses.
Or her strange shoes.
It's the way she acts that really gets us.
Ms Frizzle makes us grow green mould
on old pieces of bread.
She makes us build clay models of rubbish dumps,
draw diagrams of plants and animals,
and read five science books a week.

Other classes go on trips to the zoo,
or even the circus.
Guess where we went on our class trip.
To the waterworks!

And to get ready for the trip,
Ms Frizzle made us
spend a whole month in the library.
We had to find out exactly
how our city gets its water —
down to the last drop.
We also had to collect
ten interesting facts about water.

I DON'T THINK THERE ARE TEN INTERESTING FACTS ABOUT WATER.

MAYBE FOUR AND A HALF.

WATER FACT 1
by Wanda

About 2/3 of your body is made up of water.

Water Fact 2
by Tim

Water is the only
substance that
is found in the
form of a liquid,
a solid, _and_
a gas in nature.

LIQUID (WATER)

SOLID (ICE)

GAS
(WATER VAPOUR)

OH NO!
NOT THE
OCTOPUS
DRESS!

LET'S PRETEND
WE DON'T
KNOW HER.

In the car park,
the old school bus was waiting.
To our surprise,
there was no bus driver.
Instead, The Friz herself
was behind the wheel.

At the end of the street,
the bus went into a dark tunnel.
When we came out, something amazing
had happened.
The bus looked a lot different.
We looked different, too.
Everyone was wearing
a scuba diving outfit!
Even Ms Frizzle.

I WANT
MY MUMMY.

WATER FACT 3
by Shirley
There is water in the air you are breathing.
You can't see it, because it is in the form of an invisible gas called water vapour.
When water _evaporates_, it changes from a liquid to a gas and rises into the air.

I DIDN'T KNOW THAT!

WE'RE GOING UP!

Ms Frizzle was the only one
who didn't seem to notice the change.
She just drove on.
In the middle of a bridge,
the bus started ...

to rise into ...

Then Ms Frizzle did
the strangest thing ever.
She told everybody to get
out of the bus!
The kids didn't want to go.
But Frizzie threatened to give
extra homework if we didn't.

I'LL TAKE THE HOMEWORK.

Some kids stuck their heads
out of the cloud and looked down.
There were mountains down there!
And the cloud was going higher
every minute.

Before long, each kid was
the size of a raindrop.
In fact, each kid was
in a raindrop.
The drops began to fall.
Ms Frizzle's class was raining!

In no time, we reached
the reservoir
that holds water
for our city.
We were going into
the water purification system.
This class trip was
not so boring after all!

EVERGREEN TREES KEEP DUST AND LEAVES FROM BLOWING INTO THE RESERVOIR.

FENCE KEEPS PEOPLE AND ANIMALS FROM DIRTYING THE RESERVOIR.

THIS IS GREAT!

WHAT'S THAT?

ALUM

YUCK!

WATCH OUT FOR THE GLOBS!

MIXING BASIN

SETTLING BASIN

The water in the reservoir
was pretty dirty.
We were covered with dirt and mud.
"Follow me to the mixing basin,"
shouted Ms Frizzle.
In the mixing basin, a clumping substance
called alum was added to the water.
The alum formed globs,
and all the dirt and mud stuck
to the globs.

"On to the settling basin!"
ordered The Friz.
There the globs sank to the bottom,
and the clean water flowed off the top.
Now we were on our way to the filter.

WE CAN'T GET THROUGH!

WE'LL BE STUCK IN THE WATERWORKS FOREVER!

OUCH!

This was the sand-and-gravel filter that takes out any impurities still in the water. We were impurities, we couldn't get through! Luckily, Ms Frizzle showed us a special way around the filter. When the water came out of the filter, it was sparkling clear.

WATER FACT 7
by MOLLY

Clear water is not always clean water. It may still contain disease germs that can make you sick.

In the pipe from the filter to a storage tank, a chemical called chlorine was added to the water. Chlorine kills any remaining disease germs. A trace of fluoride was also added to keep kids from getting so many holes in their teeth.

The water had come all the way through the purification system. We thought our class trip was over. But Frizzie had other ideas. "Everybody into the storage tank," she shouted.

FLUORIDE

CHLORINE

WATER FACT 8
by Amanda Jane
The first pipes were made of hollowed-out logs.
Today pipes are made of concrete, metal, even plastic.

Before we knew what was happening, we were whooshed out of the tank and into a pipe that carries water to our city.

METAL

CONCRETE

PLASTIC

WHERE'S THE BUS?

FOLLOW ME, CLASS.

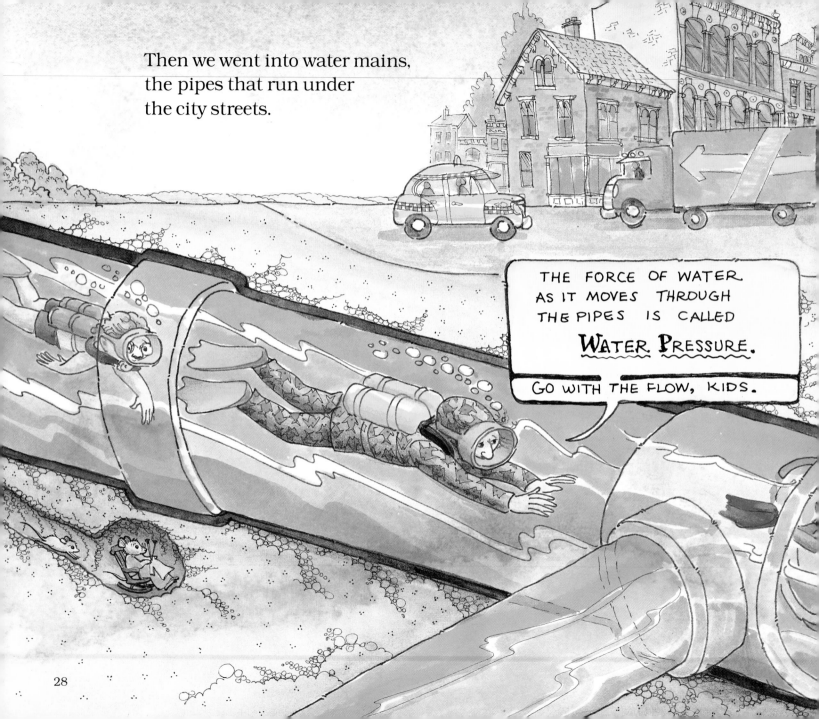

Then we went into water mains, the pipes that run under the city streets.

THE FORCE OF WATER AS IT MOVES THROUGH THE PIPES IS CALLED **WATER PRESSURE.**

GO WITH THE FLOW, KIDS.

A smaller pipe carried us to a building. We went up into the pipes in the walls.

EEEEK!

When a fourth-former
turned on a tap
in the girls' toilets,
we came splashing out.
The building was our school!
We were back!
We were our regular size again!
We were dressed in normal clothes again!
(Except for Ms Frizzle, of course.)

Back in the classroom,
Ms Frizzle acted as if
nothing strange had happened.
She started feeding the class lizard.
And she put us to work right away.
We had to make a chart
showing how water gets
to the homes and buildings
in our city.

DOWN, GIRL.

ZZZZ

When Arnold drew a picture of
a kid inside a raindrop,
Ms Frizzle said,
"Where do you *get* these
crazy ideas, Arnold?"

1
WATER EVAPORATES FROM LAKES, RIVERS, AND OCEANS.

2
CLOUDS OF WATER VAPOUR FORM IN SKY.

3
RAIN FALLS TO EARTH. SOME FALLS INTO STREAMS.

4
SOME STREAMS RUN INTO CITY'S RESERVOIR.

5
IN MIXING BASIN DIRT AND MUD STICK TO ALUM CLUMPS.

6
IN SETTLING BASIN, CLUMPS OF ALUM AND DIRT SINK TO BOTTOM.

ALUM

RESERVOIR

MIXING BASIN

SETTLING BASIN

34

Here is how our water chart turned out.

Later that day,
we saw the old bus
in the school car park.
How did *that* get there?
Did we only imagine going through
the water supply system?
Would we ever find out
what *really* happened?

THE LAST TIME
I SAW THAT BUS,
IT WAS IN A CLOUD
...I THINK...

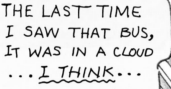

Ms Frizzle says we'll be studying
volcanoes next.
This makes us all
feel a little nervous!
After all, with a teacher
like Ms Frizzle,
anything can happen.

VOLCANO

THERE AREN'T ANY
VOLCANOES AROUND
HERE, ARE THERE?

NOTES FROM THE AUTHOR
(FOR *SERIOUS* STUDENTS ONLY)

The following notes are for serious students who do not like any kidding around when it comes to science facts. If you read these pages, you will be able to tell which facts in this book are true, and which were put in by the author as jokes. (This will also help you decide when to laugh while reading this book.)

On page 8: The green mould that grows on old bread is actually made up of tiny one-celled plants. It *cannot* talk or make any sound whatever.

On page 9: Plants do *not* have hands, *nor* do they wear sunglasses, and the soil does *not* contain hamburgers, chips, or milk shakes.

On page 13: Going through a dark tunnel will *not* cause you to wear a scuba diving outfit.

On pages 14-15: The force of gravity keeps a bus firmly on the ground. It *cannot* rise into the air and enter a cloud, no matter how much you want to miss school that day.

On pages 16-31: Children *cannot* shrink and enter raindrops, fall into streams, or pass through the water purification system. And boys and girls *cannot* come out of the taps in the girls' toilets. (Anyone knows boys are not allowed in there.)

On pages 34-35: Your town or city may not get its water from a mountain reservoir, and the purification process may be slightly different from the one in this book. Many towns get water from rivers, lakes, or wells. Do you know where your water comes from and how it is purified?

On page 36: Once a bus is left behind in a cloud, it *cannot* suddenly appear in the school car park all by itself. Obviously, someone has to go back to the cloud and drive it home.